Coping With Grief

A Self-Help Guide

(Courtesy of http://www.heavensangel.net)

C.A. Komar

ISBN: 0-7596-6967-8

This book is printed on acid free paper.

1stBooks - rev. 12/10/01

Prepared for those suffering the loss of a loved one.

*****Dedicated to the memory of my loving wife, Arlene*****

Acknowledgments

I would like to recognize the contributions of three special people who were helpful in the accomplishment of this publication:

Samuel Santoro, Jr, Ph.D, Psychologist
for his recommendations and encouragement
to develop such a worthy project.

Candice Komar, Esquire and daughter, for
her advice and guidance in the development
of the self-help theme

Mara Dean, Petroleum Engineer, and very special friend who first introduced me to spiritual works and who reviewed and edited the publication for printing

A heartfelt thanks is extended to all of them.

PREFACE

This book is a written account of the activities that I have pursued and the readings that I have acquired in order to cope with the severe grief accompanying the loss of my wife of 40 years. I was not prepared to endure such pain. Later, I discovered that no one ever is. Furthermore, there is not any readily accessible knowledge on what to expect or what to do when such tragedies happen. So, I set out to find out what works in order to restart the rest of my life. Perhaps, it is destiny that my journey through life should include the painful experience that results from the sudden and unexpected loss of a dear and lovely spouse. Having said that, it follows that part of my personal healing was to reach out to others by writing about my experience. This self-help guide is the result.

My training in science and engineering prepared me for a career in research and it is ironic that this methodology is now being used in a post-career endeavor to investigate ways to cope with grief. My efforts led to the observation, evaluation, analysis, and the documentation of what was learned. Much of the new information emerging in the literature comes from spiritual books that address the increasing demands for knowledge beyond simply believing "life is a mystery" and only faith is required to cope with tragedies. Accordingly, this guide was developed as a means to provide hope and an understanding for those who must endure the same painful process. It is a living, dynamic, document that is intended to grow and change as new information comes to light, which may be helpful to the reader and contribute to an even broader understanding of the spiritual world. At a time when knowledge of the spiritual world is receiving the attention of the general public, I found it both timely and comforting to increase my awareness on this matter and believe that others could be helped as well.

The lessons learned from my experiences indicate that the mental part of a mourner's preparedness can only be achieved with a healthy body and mind. Bereavement often includes an assault to the physical well-being of those grieving the loss of a loved one. Each individual is responsible for making an effort to restore his/her body to health once again, and then to develop his/her spiritual knowledge on life. One has to be eager to learn and to work at acquiring the knowledge that ultimately will make one better prepared to handle the challenges that await all of us in our journey through this "learning laboratory called earth." This cannot be done for you nor be acquired without a sincere, deliberate, and conscious effort on your part. You must want to survive, and to continue on life's journey until God calls your name so that your soul can be made more pure before returning to heaven in the life hereafter. I hope and pray that all who use this book will consider it as a guide toward acquiring the spiritual knowledge that I think is the food of life.

God Bless You All

"One has to be eager to

acquire the knowledge

for handling the

challenges in life"

CONTENTS

"There is a spiritual awakening

in the world

and a thirst for knowledge

on the afterlife"

Book Notes for Recommended Readings

- **Knowledge of the Spiritual World is Emerging**

- **Healing of the Soul is Necessary to Gain Acceptance into the Eternal World**

- **Death is Not the End of the Spirit's Journey, Simply a Graduation from Earth's School**

Recognizing the Symptoms of Grief

Grief is the combination of sorrow, strong emotion, and the resulting confusion that comes from losing someone important to you. Not only do you mourn the loss of that person, but also you mourn for yourself. Furthermore, the more love that was shared makes the time for healing a little longer. How we deal with the grief that follows the death of a loved one is a very private and unique individual process. It is important to let every person experience the grief process on his or her own timeline. This may take years. It is also important to know that once you have entered the healing process, feelings of grief may come and go at different times, especially on memorable occasions and holidays.

Much has been written on dealing with the loss of a loved one and it is the intent of this narrative to share with all the "classic stages" of grief; namely, *shock, denial, anger, guilt, depression,* and *acceptance.*

Shock is often the first reaction upon learning the loss of a loved one. It is very common to feel numb all over. This is how your body instinctively reacts to pain. It is not unreasonable to experience tightness in the chest or throat, difficulty breathing, irritability, muscle weakness, lack of energy, dry mouth, and /or trouble eating and sleeping. This is a time to consult your physician for medication to help with the grief.

Denial often quickly follows shock. It is not uncommon to say, "I don't believe this", or "this is not happening to me". You may also find yourself searching for your loved one. The forms of searching may vary from dreams that seem as real as life, and imagination caused by familiar sounds, smells, and sights. These may come when you least expect them, and are an important way for adjusting to your loss. Counselors are typically needed to help you change your lifetime patterns, or routines to cope with this. Most often the importance of such modifications of one's lifestyle are overlooked.

Anger is a part of the healing process that involves a period of intense emotion. Everyone is expected to experience this emotion. It's simply OK to do so. You may find yourself angry at a situation, or at a person. You may be mad at God, or you may be mad at the deceased for the actions that may have been taken or not taken. This is a normal and natural response to the loss of control death imposes upon us. We simply want to find a reason and place blame, either on ourselves or on those around us.

Guilt can be triggered by almost anything, but usually comes from the feeling that "I could have, I should have, I wish I would have, etc." This is known as "survivor's guilt" and is the term used for expressing the feelings of those left behind who typically blame themselves for the loss of a loved one. Experts advise that exercise is an excellent stress reliever and frequent exercise is a must to help the healing process.

Depression is common after the loss of a loved one. You may lose interest in many activities, especially those you shared. Some symptoms of depression include loss of appetite, lethargy, isolation, and self-pity.

Trained professionals are available to help you cope with your loss and ensuing depression. Your physician can be a source of relief by prescribing anti-depressant medication to assist in the healing of your body, and a counselor can offer guidance on therapy to follow. Often joining a bereavement group can be a good thing to do. In such groups, one can have the opportunity to discuss one's feeling with others if it helps to do so. However, this approach may not be for those who wish to cope with their grief in private. Furthermore, this is not a forum for those who are seeking information and some understanding of reasons to accept life's setbacks.

Acceptance of the loss is inevitable but this takes time, and time seems to stand still whenever you need for it to pass faster. Talking through your feelings and memories can be therapeutic for some in reaching acceptance. Although it does not seem possible at first, there will come a time in the future when you can think about your loved one with fond memories, and without any feelings of guilt, anger, or sadness. This will come when you allow yourself time and give yourself permission to experience bereavement in its entirety. Finally, increasing your knowledge of the spiritual world is a source of comfort. It is an attempt to gain some insight on what life is all about. Knowledge on the subject is now available in bookstores and on the Internet that addresses the increasing quest for information beyond faith alone wherein it is believed "life is a mystery." Together, reasoning relative to the purpose of life on earth coupled with strength from one's faith, appears to be a more formidable approach in arriving at acceptance of fact.

What Can Be Expected in Coping with Grief?

Much has been written in the literature and on the Internet relative to expectations of grief. Most of this literature provides lessons learned from the experiences of others. Others focus on the practical approaches to diagnose what symptoms of grief are likely to be present. Essentially, you can expect that grief will:

—take longer than most people think

—require more energy than you would have imagined

—involve many changes

—evolve in all spheres of your life (psychological, spiritual & physical)

Furthermore, your grief will:

—entail mourning for all the unfulfilled expectations in life

—involve a wide variety of feelings and reactions

—resurrect old issues, feelings, and unresolved conflicts from the past

Finally, you will experience:

—identity confusion

—lack of self-esteem

—trouble thinking and making decisions

—upsurges in grief over certain dates, and events

—questioning your religion and philosophy of life

How Long Does it Take to Get Through the Grieving Process?

Generally, it has been reported in the literature that 18 to 24 months is typical just to stabilize yourself after the death of a loved one. It can take much longer when the death was a violent one. The worst times are said to be after 4 to 7 months have elapsed whenever the shock or numbness has subsided. Then you need to take action to get help to get through the grieving process. Essentially, you might consider:

—talking with a true friend or others who have been there and survived

—taking time to lament, to experience being a victim

—allowing yourself the opportunity to cry and to experience the pain

—reaching out and trying to help others in some small way

—deepening your faith in God, in yourself, and in others

Constructive Steps for Coping with Grief

It is stated many times in the literature that grief is not a sign of weakness but is necessary to bearing sorrow honestly and accepting reality; i.e., a change has occurred.

It should also be recognized that grief is an inevitable tribute to the loss of someone very precious. One cannot run away from it nor repress it without suffering both physically and mentally. For most people there is a pattern of constructive steps that may be followed to guide us through the process.

Essentially, these include the following:

- Consult your physician to get assistance in coping with anxiety and depression

—medication to reduce anxiety and permit one to sleep

—medication to fight depression so that crying can be controlled

—guidance to combat stress and its complications

- Develop an exercise-training program to control stress (physician approved)

—join a fitness center and conduct hour long cardiovascular therapy (often)
—walk for thirty-minute periods (three days per week)
—take the initiative to start new ventures (hiking, biking, etc)

- Follow a diet to maintain health

—using a menu of soups and salads
—low fat products, lean meat and fish
—lots of fruits, vegetables, and water daily

- Consult a counselor to complement healing

—seek guidance on changes required to avoid painful memories

—seek measures to complement the medical physician's plan

- Investigate the mystery of life through spiritual readings

—understand that life itself is an earthly experience for us spiritual beings

—rely on faith for healing of the soul and gaining acceptance to the eternal world

—recognize that death is not the end of the spirit's journey, merely a transition

Spiritual Readings To Investigate The Meaning Of Life

Knowledge of the Spiritual World Is Emerging

1. Bodine, Echo L. *Echoes of the Soul: The Soul's Journey Beyond the Light, Through Life, Death, and Life after Death,* New World Library 1999, 173pp.

2. Browne, Sylvia. *The Other Side and Back: The Psychic's Guide to Our World and Beyond,* Dutton Books, 1999, 279pp.

3. Freeman, Sidney L. *Life after Death: A Survey of the Cumulative Evidence,* Kroshka Books, 1998, 251 pp.

4. Zukav, Gary. *Soul Stories,* Simon & Schuster, 2000, 256pp.

Healing of the Soul is Necessary for Acceptance into the Eternal World

5. Anderson, George and Andrew Barone. *Lessons from the Light: Extraordinary Messages on Comfort and Hope from the Other Side,* Putnam, 1999, 321pp.

6. Van Praagh. *Healing Grief: Reclaiming Life After Any Loss,* Dutton, 2000, 224pp.

7. Zukav, Gary. *The Seat of the Soul,* Simon & Schuster, 1989, 248 pp.

Death is Not the End of the Spirit's Journey, Simply a Graduation from Earth's School

8. Guggenheim, Wm, and Judy Guggenheim. *Hello from Heaven,* Bantam Books, 1997, 398pp.

9. Margolis, Char. *Questions from Earth; Answers from Heaven,* St. Martins Press. 1999, 241pp.

10. Shockey, Peter. *Reflections of Heaven,* Doubleday, 1999, 240pp.

11. Van Praagh, James. *Talking to Heaven,* Signet Book, 1999, 292pp.

12. Van Praagh, James. *Reaching to Heaven: A Spiritual Journey Through Life and Death,* Dutton, 1999, 191pp.

"Souls exist on earth to heal

themselves so that

they can subsequently gain

acceptance to the

eternal world"

BOOK NOTES

The information that follows is a series of Book Notes that summarize what the references are about and what I gathered from reading them. The Booknotes includes synopses from the books relative to what the author and/or publisher expect the reader to encounter in the readings and what I personally learned from reading them.

Furthermore, the Booknotes also include the reasons why I am recommending these books to others in the process of healing from the loss of a loved one. The topics were recent publications that seemed to corroborate what each author wants to convey in building a thorough knowledgebase on the understanding of life itself. These books are available in most local bookstores or on the Internet.

The first four books (Spiritual Readings 1 to 4) are the most recent references on the fact that there is a spiritual awakening in the world and a thirst for more knowledge on the subject. There are hundreds of books on religion and spiritualism in the open literature but I believe that the ones that I have chosen provide a solid framework from which to begin. Their consensus view provides overwhelming indications that people want to know more about life itself. Psychic Sylvia Browne is currently enjoying increased exposure on spiritual guides and angels and appears regularly on talk shows.

The next three books (Spiritual Readings 5 to 7) provide the evidence or arguments that souls exist on earth to heal themselves so that they can subsequently gain acceptance to the eternal world. This is by design and is not easy. Each soul must plan and accept a blueprint that governs his ventures on earth until soul purification is accomplished. In particular, authors Van Praagh and Zukav have emerged as authorities offering constructive guidance through the steps of the grieving process. Both appear frequently on many talk shows as well.

The remaining five books (Spiritual Readings 8 to 12) provide sufficient evidence to feel comfort in the belief that death is not so final after all, and that our spirits simply graduate from the school of life on earth to perform duties in the next dimensions of time and space. These references cite after-death communications that occur in various forms; e.g., sensing a presence, hearing a voice, feeling a touch, smelling a fragrance, visual experiences, telephone calls, and unexplainable electrical disturbances in lights, appliances, and energy forms. All of these offer comfort to those of us who have suffered a loss in that we are not alone and will someday re-unite with our loved ones.

BOOK NOTE NO. 1

Bodine, Echo L. *Echoes of the Soul: The Soul's Journey Beyond the Light, Through Life, Death and Life after Death,* New World Library, 1999, 173pp.

This book is a heartwarming and enlightening discussion of the existence of the spiritual world that we all have yet to experience. The author provides a vision of our souls and the journey that they take through life, death, and life after death. It provides a new understanding of life, and provides the intellectual reader a deep sense of peace, or serenity at the very core of being.

The reader is made aware that everyone has a soul, which is made up of energy that comes from God. The soul takes on the appearance of the body that it's living within. There is a voice within every soul that guides it through its lifetimes. This is commonly referred to as intuition. Souls are attached to the physical bodies via silver cords, which are severed only at the time of death. Nevertheless, the soul has the ability to come and go from the body at will. This usually occurs via the astral projection and out of body experiences that are often talked about.

In an attempt to enlighten us as to the world around us, the author describes life in heaven and the different levels of the soul starting with level one (characterized as totally self-absorbed) through level five (wherein one understands what life and God are all about).

Life is considered the "school on earth" where souls are sent to achieve sufficient wisdom and the desired state of perfection required for achieving eternal life. Those who believe in heaven, angels, and life after death will be intrigued by this well written book that attempts to answer the question—"why am I here?"

This book is for those who wish to know more about who we are, our life in this world, and where we will go when we die. It is easy to understand, and leaves you with a more comforting feeling about life and death. After reading, one achieves a greater sense of appreciation for life itself and renewed enthusiasm for living life fully. It rekindles your faith in God, provides a sense of inner peace, and makes the reader want more and more information.

Personally, I have always been interested in stories of life after death, souls, spirits, and heaven. Furthermore, I have always wondered if there was more to life than the here and now. Having lost my spouse, I have been searching for more answers on life after death. This book made the events that I experienced more understandable, but not easier to accept. Nevertheless, it was a first step in coming to grips with life's most tragic moments.

BOOK NOTE NO. 2

Browne, Sylvia. *The Other Side and Back: A Psychic's Guide to Our World and Beyond.* Dutton Books, 1999, 279 pp.

This book is very helpful in the understanding of the other side of the thinly veiled world, which is called the fourth dimension. Whether you believe all that the author has to say or not, this book provides provoking thoughts about the afterlife. No one truly knows what lies ahead, but each of us has the need to search for our own meaning and focus in life.

For the most part, the author knows that God is alive and well. He has created us, loves us constantly, eternally, and unconditionally. He is as much a part of us as our parents, grandparents, and everyone else in our ancestry. Furthermore, the author advocates that the other side, and the spirits that live there, are as real as the earth we live on. The only thing separating "here" from "there" is a small difference in vibration frequency.

We are taught that we spirits leave the other side to come to earth, for the purpose of experiencing and overcoming negativity and learning from it in an ongoing process of spiritual perfection. We choose who and what we'll be before we come here, and we even write our own blueprint to chart exactly what we want to accomplish on this brief trip away from home. We're always surrounded by spirit guides, angels, departed loved ones, and God himself to help us. We simply must learn how to ask for help. One of the lessons we learn is the role of angels and spiritual guides and how they communicate with us and how we nuture them. Another lesson is learned from dreams where "releases" are subconscious dealings with unfinished work, where "wishes" are typically needs for more intimacy in your life, and where "precognition" dreams are insights into your blueprint future.

This wise and empowering book offers practical advice, clear guidance, and heartfelt assurances during an eye-opening journey into other worlds. It is an invaluable handbook for spiritual survival in the new millennium.

Reading Sylvia's book opened my eyes and heart to things that I previously considered coincidences and random events (like electrical disturbances in household lights and communications devices including phones, TVs, and radios). My interest was further enhanced after seeing her appear on various talk shows and monthly on the Montel Williams show. I personally believe that none of us truly knows what lies ahead and we need to search for our own meaning and purpose in life. Sylvia's version is a very optimistic one, and left me with a more positive outlook as I awaken each new day.

BOOK NOTE NO. 3

Freeman, Sidney L. *Life After Death: A Survey of the Cumulative Evidence,* Kroshka Books, 1998, 251pp.

The author undertook a detailed examination and analysis of documented evidence to determine whether communication with the dead was possible. If death is indeed an experience not to be feared, and is merely a painless, peaceful transition from one phase to another, then it was important to be revealed to the general public; hence, this book was written.

Notwithstanding the numerous obstacles, frustration and disbelief of many, the author concludes that there is sufficient evidence to state that life after death is a scientific fact.

The cumulative evidence shows that the soul and the spirit constitute an exact counterpart of the physical body. The second body is invisible and intangible to us because of its lesser density, just like air. When death occurs, the soul leaves the expired physical body, but accompanying the soul are the mind, memory, consciousness, and personality of the individual. These survive death and enter into the next phase of existence. There, a new and intriguing active life continues, but with different motivations and lifestyle.

Knowledge of the facts of death are more important than the facts of life because the uninformed can be made aware of the things that lead to a beautiful life in the future.

A wondrous life awaits the decent person but for those who choose a different course, at least they will be forewarned. The only hope for man, according to the spiritual forces, is to have a pre-knowledge of what happens to us after we die and what the ultimate purpose in life is all about. One of the most important messages from departed loved ones is that your prayers for their well-being and spiritual progress are extremely appreciated and help their advancement.

The spirit forces have concluded that the Earth and its earthpeople are not yet ready for a full and complete disclosure. Therefore, the knowledge of man must be raised by slow stages, beginning with the things that they know and then leading to what they do not know. The evidence documented by the author and his personal experiences with mediums and psychics indicate that a far different world lies in wait for each and every one of us when we die. You will find that you will be alive when you depart this life. You will have your mind, your memory, your consciousness, and a spirit body. You will find that death is not the end of life but rather is a commencement—a graduation to a higher school of learning. Caring guides will direct you to future choices for new studies, occupations, and advancement to the higher planes. Transition should not be feared but welcomed. When it's time to leave the Earth, give thanks to God, whose beneficial plan provides so wonderful a place for the next step.

I felt that this book corroborates what authors Bodine and Browne have said and provides much in the way of anecdotal evidence to support their views. There are so many stories to make you believe that what psychics see and tell is true. Theirs is a gift from God to help us to grow gradually in wisdom and understanding on life on earth.

BOOK NOTE NO. 4

Zukav, Gary. *Soul Stories,* Simon & Schuster, 2000. 256pp.

Gary Zukav uses stories as the best way to explain every idea since the beginning of time. In his previous best seller, "Seat of the Soul," he explains his basic beliefs and provides details about authentic empowerment and how to reach beyond our current senses. Through "Soul Stories," he promotes the belief that the universe is alive and that God is present in our lives. He advocates that we are individual souls sent to earth to fulfill a task, or to learn lessons that will benefit us in the next life. His fundamental assertion is that we are to view life as a school and that we are here to learn. The book is more of a meditation aide than an information source. His message is to practice kindness and what you express will be experienced in harmony, trust, and love. If you keep your mind open and aware at all times, you will probably find that every story has a message for you.

The author writes openly and intimately about negative periods of his life when he felt jealousy, competitiveness, fear, anger, and all the other emotions we encounter. Furthermore, he talks about how his understanding of these emotions changed as he awakened to the recognition of a Universe that is alive and compassionate. This book is filled with stories that show how such concepts as intuition, harmony, sharing, and forgiveness actually express themselves in the lives of people. There are fifty-two stories in this book that can be a spiritual lift for each week of the year.

I found that this book did an excellent job in raising an awareness of the need to nuture our souls. It is up to the readers to find their own way on the journey through life. God created our souls and can lead us on the path to the truth. Both the "Seat of the Soul" and "Soul Stories" need to be read in order to comprehend the philosophy advocated by

Zukav. Each page needs to be savored and personal conclusions need to be advanced so that you can identify with your own spiritual stories and gain a more thorough understanding of them. This knowledge will help spread ideas about enlightenment and living beyond just survival to a large audience. In particular, this book helps people look inside themselves for inner truth and what is most important to them in their lives.

BOOK NOTE NO. 5

Anderson, George, and Andrew Barone. *George Anderson's Lessons from the Light:* Extraordinary Messages of Comfort and Hope from the Other Side, *Putnam,1999, 321pp.*

This book is about the author's experience as a medium for communicating with departed souls. It is a detailed account of what happens in the hereafter life. His description of the afterworld comes straight from the understanding of what souls on the other side tell him. After reading it, you will acquire a comforting message of hope for anyone suffering the loss of a loved one.

Anderson writes that no one can speak as clearly about coping with loss as the souls that have passed over to the afterlife. They have a fresh and direct way of helping those left behind to understand that physical death is just a means to a greater end. The spirits talk to the author about their world and ours with such an attitude that you feel that they are happy and at peace. Their words help us to look differently at our world here on earth and the reasons why we must continue on our spiritual journey.

The most important message coming from the spiritual world beyond is that we are all on a spiritual journey on earth to learn lessons. We were already told that the lessons would be many and difficult. Whatever we need to learn, e.g. courage, patience, forgiveness of others, is part of our destiny as family and the career of our life's work. It is all for the purpose of learning from knowledge, the pain, and the struggle in this lifetime so that we can benefit from it in the life hereafter.

The author feels that the communication he has experienced as a medium has helped families cope with the pain of their physical loss. They know that someday, we will all be reunited, and while they don't feel the pain of separation as we do, they recognize our pain and try to help us cope with it. However, theirs is a constant reminder that the journey is ours to walk until it leads to them on the other side. Often, these souls communicate to the author that they will be there as "guardian angels" to assist us along the way.

It is my view that George Anderson has a gift that allows him to communicate with souls that have passed on. The peace and love that evolve from such communications is the result of hearing specific details about the departed souls that no one could possibly know other than the family. There are no works to describe the comfort and sense of peace that comes from reading the accounts of his experiences. This book is excellent and can really help anyone to understand and to cope with the unthinkable, which is the loss of a loved one.

BOOK NOTE NO. 6

Van Praagh, James. *Healing Grief: Reclaiming Life After Any Loss,* Penguin Audiobooks. 2000.

This book offers great comfort in the loss of a loved one through death. The author gently reminds us that we need to grieve in our own way and in our own time. All grief needs to be felt and realized even though our society tends to hasten the process and does not seem to respect that each of us must have time to heal. What really makes this book interesting comes from the inspirational stories experienced by grieving families who have sought the advice of the psychic author. Loved ones have come through from the other side and provided personal information that have helped the grieving ones overcome their illness. Once a person can overcome his or fear of death, life can become more meaningful, less stressful, and much more enjoyable.

The reader gets reassurance and hope from the message that we will someday be reunited with our loved ones. The first two books published by the author were food for thought and were very uplifting. This book has practical, insightful guidelines for not only moving through grief but learning how to become a better person. This is an important book not only for those suffering a recent loss, but also for those who have not properly grieved a loss from the past. Identifiable steps for dealing with grief helps a great deal, and prepares those seeking knowledge to be better prepared to deal with losses in the future.

In particular, this book teaches that the soul lives on after death and one day you will meet your loved ones again. *Healing Grief* will remind you that you are not alone. The author reminds us that each soul is on a unique path and when that soul's mission is accomplished, the soul returns home to heaven and continues to live in the afterlife. It is just the physical body that exists no more. Van Praagh opens your mind to the knowledge that life after death is real and that one can stay in touch with our departed during our life here on earth. It is a must read for anyone who has experienced a loss. It will help you cope with your pain and anger, and to get on with the rest of your life. As a result, you can develop a better appreciation for the compassion and understanding that one must acquire in order to help yourself and others.

Personally, I found this book to be interesting and as I begin to apply the words and wisdom to my own situation with a recent personal loss, I feel that I am gaining a better perspective of the grieving process that must accompany it. This book has offered me the knowledge and the strength to get through a very difficult period of pain.

BOOK NOTE NO. 7

Zukav, Gary. *The Seat of the Soul,* Simon & Schuster, 1989, 248pp.

The author believes that humans are immortal souls first, and physical beings second while on earth. This insightful synthesis of modern psychology and new-age principles has been described as the "physics of the soul." He advocates that once we become aware of this transformation sequence, then we will stimulate our spiritual growth and become better people in the process. In this book, he explains why increased sensory perception will mark the next phase of human evolution, how the choices we make can change our existence, and what we can do to have more compassion, trust, and understanding. The message of this book is that our life has a purpose and this journey on earth is to now align our personalities with our souls. It is to create harmony, cooperation, sharing, and reverence for life itself.

In particular, if one desires to know his/her soul, the first step to recognize is that you have a soul. When the energy of the soul is recognized, acknowledged, and valued, it begins to infuse the life of the personality. While each of us is on earth, every experience that we have aligns the personality with the soul. The understanding of this requires a sense beyond the five that we have been given on earth. Our journey on earth will ultimately lead us to the multi-sensory perception required to understand what life is all about. He illustrates how the emerging values of the spirit changes marriages into spiritual partnerships, psychology into spiritual psychologists, and transforms our lives everyday.

This is a thought-provoking book and is sometimes hard to understand because the author tries to show that the linkage of the spiritual with physical processes has a foundation for understanding in the physics of the world. This book, to me, says that we can all make the world a better place to live and to work by making a conscious effort to make it that way. I appreciated the insights into how to have a greater vision of everyday life experiences. This book turned out to be a practical, down to earth guide to self-discovery. As a result, one can acquire an appreciation for how life can become much more loving, fun, easy, and satisfying. Personally, the best way to get the most of his message is to listen to the audio tape of the book after you have already read it. The time will be well worth it and will elevate your mind to a better level of understanding so that when more of the same is talked about on the networks, the more you will be prepared to follow it.

BOOK NOTE NO. 8

Guggenheim, William, and Judy Guggenheim. *Hello from Heaven,* Bantam Books, 1997, 398pp

This book reports on the study of a new field of research called After-Death Communication. It is about a spiritual experience that occurs when a person is contacted directly by a family member or friend who has died. Included within are 350 first-hand accounts of those whose lives have been changed by messages or signs from the deceased and these spiritual experiences offer hope, love, and comfort for thousands of people.

The authors describe the accounts of After-Death Communication in twelve different forms and these occur without the aid of psychics, or mediums. They are the following:

Sensing a Presence: This is the most common form of contact. It is a distinct feeling that your loved one is nearby, even though he or she can't be seen or heard.

Hearing A Voice: Some people state they hear a voice, however, the majority of communications are by telepathy—in your mind.

Feeling A Touch: A perceived pat, caress, stroke, kiss or even a hug are all forms of affection, nuturing and love.

Smelling A Fragrance: Smelling a favorite cologne, perfume or some other common aroma may give you a sense of closeness with the departed loved one.

Visual Experiences: Appearances range from a "transparent mist" to "absolutely solid" and may occur in the bedroom, in the car, or even on a plane. Typically, these sightings will be joyous and provide a sense of well being in the afterlife.

Visions: Typically pictures of departed loved ones appear as a two-dimensional slide or as a three-dimensional hologram and are in radiant colors.

Twilight Experiences: These occur as you're falling asleep, waking up, meditating or praying. All of these are possible in this state of consciousness.

Experiences While Asleep: Sleep state communications are much more vivid, intense, colorful, and real than dreams. Both one-way and two-way communications are typical.

Out of Body Experiences: They are dramatic experiences during which you leave your body and often visit your loved one at the place or level where he or she exists.

Telephone Calls: Sometimes people will hear a phone ringing and your loved one may leave you a short message. The voice may be clear but seem far away.

Physical Phenomena: Bereaved people often experience lights blinking, radios and televisions being turned on or off, photographs being moved, and a lot a things that have an effect of a "bump during the night."

Symbolic Communication: often people ask a Higher Power for a sign that the departed still exists. Common signs include butterflies, rainbows, flowers or coins and pictures.

Personally, I found great comfort in learning that our departed ones and the love they have for us continue beyond this life and place. Furthermore, to know that they desire to communicate with us is a true joy and uplift of the heart. It almost seems that if you look for such signs, you can become a receiver of messages of various sorts. (Note: While I was typing this review, my FAX machine rang but no message came through. Could this be a sign from beyond? I think so.) This book is a must-read, and one of a kind.

BOOK NOTE NO. 9

Margolis, Char. *Questions from Earth, Answers from Heaven,* St. Martins,1999, 241pp.

The author is a psychic and has the uncanny ability to make contact with departed spirits.

In this book, she shares her most exciting experiences and offers insights as to how to develop your own psychic abilities. Her inspiring advice can help to develop your innate ability to sense danger or to protect others. She also provides guidelines for utilizing intuition for making decisions about business, family, health and love. In particular, she shows you how to follow your intuition for the following:

—finding misplaced objects
—psychically contacting people or coincidently running into them
—choosing or changing a career
—getting a health checkup
—easing the pain from losing a loved one
—expanding your wisdom and happiness
—increasing your ability to love
—preventing problems and attaining goals your life

Margolis also talks about the lessons that we must learn from our time spent here on earth. These lessons are designed to help us evolve as souls. A few of these lessons that

are required as we progress thorough our lifetimes are listed as the following:

Lesson # 1: We are responsible for our lives. Even though some things may be predestined because we need to learn a particular lesson, there are ways to change destiny through our own efforts.

Lesson # 2: Judge not, lest ye be judged. We have a responsibility to look at all people with understanding and compassion. It's up to us to learn what separates us and to find out what makes us alike. So let go of your expectations about people and let the people you love grow in their own way. The best thing that we can give others is our love.

Lesson # 3: The secret of life is balance. Balance is the key in keeping ourselves together. It's important for us to be balanced emotionally, psychologically, physically, and psychically. When we are in balance, it is much easier to stay in tune with the highest levels of wisdom and goodness.

Lesson # 4: Change and growth are not optional. Our nature and our purpose are to keep growing and changing until we attain the highest level of wisdom that we can. Sometimes change will cause us pain and may require us to leave behind places, things, and relationships that no longer serve us.

Lesson # 5: We are all in this together. My growth will help you to grow and vice versa. We all need to pay attention to each other, and to do our best to help one another.

Lesson # 6: Use the gifts God gave you to make things better. When we learn the lesson of being our best to do the best, we will have taken a large step toward our ultimate goal of the absolute goodness, wisdom and love that is God.

Lesson #7: Contentment and gratitude make for a very rich life. Gratitude opens the heart like nothing else. When you learn the lesson of living in gratitude and contentment, your transition to the spirit world will seem easy and natural because that is the energy in which the highest spirits live all the time

BOOK NOTE NO. 10

Shockey, Peter. *Reflections of heaven: A Millennial Odyssey of Miracles, Angels, and Afterlife,* Doubleday, 1999, 240 pp.

Author Peter Shockey writes about his experiences in exploring the near-death phenomenon as a filmmaker. While filming more modern day stories of miracles, angels, and reincarnation, he began to notice a parallel with the stories of miracles, angels, and afterlife that were written about during the time of Christ's arrival on earth. In this book, the author shares the most memorable accounts that he has had over the past decade, and offers new insights into what the presence of the Divine in daily life can mean. He puts these encounters in an enlightening context as he explores patterns of Divine intervention in history as well as in the Bible.

In particular, the author captures God's fundamental truths along with universal law and relates both to the growing spirituality of the individual and collective society, as we move into the new millennium. This book is a stepping-stone on the path to enlightenment. It is written in a highly intellectual and intelligent manner so that proof and evidence that we live in a spiritual world cannot be misunderstood. There are twenty-three stories dealing with the major topics of miracles, angels, the afterlife, and millennial reflections.

After adding the historical investigations to the contemporary accounts, the author offers his belief: "*I have no alternative but to believe in the existence of a loving Creator. His compassion and intelligence is infinitely superior to our own, and He originates and operates from a wholly different plane than what we can grasp intellectually, namely that of Spirit. I am convinced that He has created an organized system for running the universe, in both the physical and spiritual realms. He has provided us with tools and opportunities for communicating with Him and obtaining help and guidance when we need it. It is not only interesting but vital to recognize patterns in both our spiritual and religious history that seem to be triggered by the millennium swing, particularly surrounding rumors of Armageddon and the end times."*

I believe that the series of stories can and will provide new insights into the world around us as we move through this journey called life on earth. They are uplifting and illuminating. Readers can acquire increased knowledge about God and the universe.

Accordingly, their faith will become an even more important part of their life.

BOOK NOTE NO. 11

Van Praagh, James. *Talking to Heaven*, Signet, 1999, 292pp.

This book offers comforting and somewhat startling stories about contacts with departed souls. In particular, the author offers spiritual and psychological help to those struggling through grief. The reader will get exposed to down-to-earth discussions of the afterlife and the role of spiritual guides in it. Most of the experiences come from helping grieving people come to terms with the loss of a loved one. He offers them a means for recognizing and dealing with the harrowing pain of grief in a healthy manner.

Most of the book focuses on the gifts that a medium, like the author, has to deploy. The first of these is mental mediumship whereby the clairvoyance, clairaudience, clairsentience, and inspirational thoughts to communicate with souls in the afterlife are utilized. The second type of mediumship is physical, and uses channeling as a well-known approach. In this manner, materialization of the spirit on the other side can appear in forms as faces or whole bodies to the medium. Such phenomena as spiritual healing and spiritual photography are used for such communication.

For me, this book continues the exploration of the other world and provides a practical guide to finding a closer connection to it. If we want to do everything to help our souls along on their eternal journeys toward enlightenment, then we must remove the emotional obstacles of guilt and fear that are inhibiting our ability to learn. After we find that we can cope with the shock, denial, anger, and acceptance, then we need to subsequently move on with our life. Even though it may not be clear right away, each of us is needed on earth to interact with others who are learning similar lessons for the good of their souls. We need to realize that the grief we experience can assist us in being a bit more sensitive to others in a similar position. We need to constantly remind ourselves that to go through such an adventure called life, we need both strength and courage.

BOOK NOTE NO. 12

Van Praagh, James. *Reaching to Heaven,* Dutton, 1999, 191pp.

The author attempts to bridge the gap between the physical and spiritual worlds by imparting knowledge received from a greater spiritual existence. Within the soul—right inside every individual—lies a whole new world of healing and hope, of familiarity, and truth. To reach it, optimum growth is developed through "soul lessons" and is exercised by a spirit's free will. These soul lessons are learned through experiences in the "schoolroom called earth."

This book is organized into three parts:

- *Part One*—The Journey
- *Part Two*—The Spirit Speaks
- *Part Three*—The Awakening

Part One discusses the starting and ending points of life on earth. Relative to this, the reader is asked to accept the fact that the spiritual soul chooses to enter earth's laboratory and to develop the attributes necessary for a higher appreciation of life in the eternal world and subsequently acceptance to it. The first concept that the reader is asked to visualize, relates to the insertion of a spiritual energy into a physical life form and together they make up who we are, how we look, and the kind of personalities that we display. As life journey progresses, our mind is awakened to the need for a commitment toward making the world a better place to live and work, and to help others grow in wisdom and love so that our learning can be completed in a peaceful environment.

Part Two talks about the myriad tests a soul must go through on this earth. These include dealing with expectations that are sometimes difficult to achieve, guilt associated with the failures that we experience in our development, fear of what's out there and God's wrath, forgiveness for mistakes that we make and that others make relative to us, and finally, love that we extend to others when we reach out to help them.

Part Three shows what happens when our souls are awakened to the attributes needed to be worthy of the kingdom of heaven. The evolving education and meditation bring out the real light in each of us which is a beacon guiding each of us to be self-respectful, responsible, self-reliant, and spiritually aware of the world around us and our role in it.

In the pursuit thereof, the virtues of patience, courage, faith, and love are combined with wisdom, creativity, joy, and laughter to create the attributes expected of the child of God.

Then, and only then, can we expect to achieve the keys to a higher life and our acceptance into a more heavenly place.

For me, “Reaching to Heaven” continues the exploration of the other world that began with the author’s best selling “Talking to Heaven” and provides a practical guide to finding a closer connection to it. If we want to do everything to help our souls along on their eternal journeys toward enlightenment, then we must remove the emotional obstacles of guilt, and fear that are blocking their paths.

"There is the belief that death

is not so final after all

and that our spirits simply

graduate from the

school of life on earth to

perform duties in the

next dimension of time and space."

A Final Thought

Life itself is a just a journey
Our time on earth is one small part
Thoughts occur of loved ones lost
Because they are with us from the start

Just think how great it would be
If we could learn some day
That nothing but our sadness
Would ever pass away

We could flourish in the afterlife
Where there are no days and years
We would welcome its comfort
And forget our sorrow and our tears

What we have learned is to love
And enjoy life every day
For knowledge learned is wisdom gained
Which will help us find our way

I'll leave you with this final thought
That no one could love too much
For all the love that was ever shown
Stays in the hearts, which were touched

C.A.Komar

ABOUT THE AUTHOR

The author is a retired civil servant who completed a successful 40-year career with the U.S. Department of Energy. After the tragic loss of my beloved wife, I set out to find out how to deal with the painful experience that results from the sudden and unexpected loss of a loved one. I feel that part of my personal healing was to reach out to others by writing about my experiences. This self-help guide is the result.

My training in science and engineering prepared me for a career in research and it is ironic that the methodology is being used in an investigative approach to discover ways to cope with grief. My efforts led to the observation, evaluation, analysis, and the documentation of what was learned. Much of the new information emerging in the literature comes from spiritual books that address the increasing demands for knowledge beyond simply believing "life is a mystery" and that only faith is required to cope with the pain and suffering from tragedies. At a time when knowledge of the spiritual world is receiving the attention of the general public, I found it both timely and comforting to increase my awareness on this matter and believe that others could be helped as well.

www.ingramcontent.com/pod-product-compliance
Ingram Content Group UK Ltd.
Pitfield, Milton Keynes, MK11 3LW, UK
UKHW040016200726
13854UKWH00001B/235

9 780759 669673